Protestant Christianity and Mental Health
Beliefs, Research and Applications

Harold G. Koenig, M.D.

Copyright © 2017 Harold G. Koenig

All rights reserved.

ISBN-13: 978-1544642109
ISBN-10: 1544642105

DEDICATION

To my daughter, Rebekah

CONTENTS

	Introduction	1
1	Christian Demography	4
2	Historical Background	6
3	Core Protestant Beliefs	12
4	Protestant Practices	21
5	Protestant Values	26
6	Christianity and Mental Health: Speculations	33
7	Christianity and Mental Health: The Research	38
8	Clinical Applications	48
9	Summary and Conclusions	54
	References	55
	Author Biography	61

INTRODUCTION

The Christian faith (both Catholic and Protestant) is a rich tradition with many aspects that link it to mental health. Christian theology emphasizes the existence of a *personal* God, one who created humans in his own image, one who humans can love and relate to, one who has emotions and feelings like they do. Christians believe that God deeply loves all humans, and has demonstrated that love by becoming human himself, and by suffering and dying on the cross to make up for their mistakes and errors that on their own humans are helpless to correct. In no other world religion does God become human specifically with the intention of suffering and dying to save humans from themselves. Christians believe that not only does God love them, but that God commands them to love each other as he loves them, and do so without conditions (even if enemies). All of these beliefs are likely to influence mental health and human relationships in profound ways that systematic research is now only beginning to discover.

The personal nature of God and especially the characteristics of God (i.e., loving, merciful, forgiving, reachable, responsive, and capable of being influenced) are what make the connection between the Christian belief system and mental health so powerful, at least potentially. It should not be surprising, then, that before the modern mental health system developed in the Western world, mental health problems were primarily addressed by Christian religious professionals. Their approach emphasized on kindness and compassion, humility, confession and forgiveness, and the encouragement of hopeful and positive attitudes and moral behaviors necessary for individual and community health and flourishing. Of course, Christian communities (and individual Christians) have not always operated by these principles and so have not always lived up to their full potential. Nevertheless, the Christian faith tradition even today has much to teach mental health professionals about how to address mental health problems in both Christians and non-Christians.

This small book is the second in a series on Christianity and mental health in Catholics[1] and Protestants. Here I focus on Protestant Christianity. First, I will briefly trace Protestantism from its roots and describe how the faith tradition evolved over time as it branched off from Catholicism (and the reasons for that separation). Next, I succinctly summarize present day Protestant beliefs, practices, and values (fully realizing the ambitiousness of such an endeavor), and the differences from Catholic theology. Third, I speculate on the possible ways that Protestant beliefs, practices and values may uniquely impact mental health (both positive and negative). Fourth, I summarize a systematic review of past quantitative research literature and provide a selective review of more recent studies on religion, spirituality and health in Christians (the majority of whom are Protestant). The purpose for this research review is to document the "evidence base" on which practical applications will be recommended. Finally, I will suggest clinical applications relevant to the treatment of Protestant Christian clients and members of Protestant congregations based on (a) the research evidence, (b) nearly 35 years of clinical experience, and (c) common sense. After a brief summary and conclusions, the book ends with an extensive list of references that have been cited in the text.

The **primary audience** for this book is mental health professionals and clergy who are frequently called upon to help Protestant Christians deal with emotional and other mental health problems. However, researchers who conduct studies in Protestant Christians, as well as healthcare systems that provide services to Protestant patients, will also find this volume useful. Finally, I think lay Christians more generally will discover that the information contained here will be both enlightening and faith enhancing. As someone who is currently a practicing Protestant Christian, I have found my own faith strengthened as I have done the research for this book. However, as a clinician and long-standing academic researcher, I acknowledge my personal biases and have tried to be as objective as possible in presenting the material here, especially for comparisons between Catholics and Protestants, and between Christianity and other world religions.

---

[1] I have examined Catholic Christianity elsewhere (see Koenig, 2017)

Please join me on a journey that I think you will find enlightening for the mind and inspiring for the soul, as well as useful for your professional work if you are someone who cares for the mental health needs of Protestant Christians.

CHAPTER 1

CHRISTIAN DEMOGRAPHY

In 2010, according to a Pew Research Center survey, there were approximately 2,184 million Christians who made up 31.4% of the world's population (Pew Research Center, 2011). The Christian faith tradition is divided into three main branches: Catholics (1,095 million[1]), Orthodox (260 million), and Protestants (800 million). In comparison, there are 1,600 million Muslims, who are the second-largest religious group in the world (23.2%). If estimates based on fertility rates are projected out to 2050, Christians will continue to make up 31.4% of the world's population, while Muslims will increase from 23.2% to 29.7% (Pew Research Center, 2015a).

Protestant Christianity is made up of a very heterogeneous group of 33,000+ denominations[2] that include traditional Protestants (9,000

---

[1] In October 2016, a reliable Catholic source reported the number to be 1,272 million (Fides, 2016)

[2] Denomination is defined by Barrett and colleagues (2001) as "an organized aggregate of worship centers or congregations of similar ecclesiastical tradition within a specific country; i.e. as an organized Christian church or tradition or religious group or community of believers, within a specific country, whose component congregations and members are called by the same denominational name in different areas, regarding themselves as one autonomous Christian church distinct from other denominations, churches and traditions" (vol. 1, page 16).

denominations), Independents (22,000 denominations), Anglicans (168 denominations), and non-traditional Christians (1,600 denominations) (Barrett et al. 2001). *Traditional Protestants* include groups such as Pentecostal, Baptist, Lutheran, Presbyterian/Reformed, Methodist, Seventh Day Adventist, etc. *Independent Protestants* are members of denominations such as African Independent, independent Apostolic and Charismatic groups, Full Gospel, Independent Baptist, independent Adventist, Orthodox, Fundamentalist, and many others. *Anglican denominations* include Anglo-Catholic, Central or Broad Church Anglican, Ecumenical, Evangelical Anglican, High Church Anglican, Low Church Anglican, mixed or plural Anglican, and others including the Episcopal Church (considered a group within the broad Anglican category). *Non-traditional Christian* denominations include Jehovah's Witness, Mormon, Christian Science, Unitarian/Universalists, and other groups that do not adhere to the historical creeds and councils of traditional Christianity (i.e., Nicene, Ephesus, etc.). Reasons for the many Protestant denominations are described by Bruce (1985). The main reason is the lack of institutional structure and tradition, particularly among conservative Protestants, which has allowed almost anyone to claim legitimate authority and attract a following (something that Catholicism with a long history of tradition is less vulnerable to).

The largest Protestant group in terms of membership worldwide are the Independents (including nondenominational Protestants) who make up 38.2% of all Protestants. Next are historically Pentecostal (10.8%), Anglican (10.6%), Lutheran (9.7%), Baptist (9.0%), United churches (various denominations) (7.2%), Presbyterian/Reformed (7.0%), Methodist (3.4%), Adventist (2.7%), and Congregationalist, Brethren, Salvation Army, and Moravian (1.4% total) (Pew Research Center, 2011). Protestants make up the majority of Christians in the U.S., with the latest data (2014) showing they make up two-thirds of the 70.6% of the population with a Christian affiliation (Pew Research Center, 2015b). There are more Protestants in the U.S. than in any other country in the world, with the Southern Baptist convention the largest U.S. Protestant denomination (Pew Research Center, 2011).

CHAPTER 2

HISTORICAL BACKGROUND

The people known as "Protestants" historically were Catholics who "protested" against Roman Catholic Church's teachings and practices, which they felt had strayed from the original teachings of Jesus Christ and his followers.[1] Those included abuses by a series of corrupt Catholic Popes who had concubines and illegitimate children as part of an uninhibited and extravagant lifestyle, funded by the poor and destitute faithful masses. Objections were particularly strong over the selling of indulgences (payments made for the forgiveness of sins) to an uneducated populace frightened by the devastating effects of the bubonic plague in Europe at the time. Jesus had said "If thou wilt be perfect, go and sell that thou hast, and give to the poor, and thou shalt have treasure in heaven…" (Matthew 19:21).[2] Jesus' disciples had "sold their possessions and goods, and parted them to all men, as every man had need" (Acts 2:45). Nowhere in the Bible did it say that money should be given to fund the immoral and

---

[1] The source of much of the historical information presented here is from Bainton et al. (2016)

[2] Unless otherwise specified, quotes in this and the next chapter are from the King James Version (KJV) of the Holy Bible (1987 printing, in the public domain). The first English version of the KJV was authorized by King James I of England in 1604, and completed in 1611, not long after the first English New Testament was translated from Latin by Protestant reformer William Tyndale in 1526.

degenerate lifestyle of the church hierarchy. There was also an increasing spirit of nationalism, where the monarchs of various countries sought to throw off the influence of the Catholic Church and the Pope, whom at that time had as much influence on politics and government as they did on theology.

The final split, which took place in stages, occurred between 1517 and 1534 A.D., was initiated by a professor at the University of Wittenberg and vicar in the Catholic Church, Martin Luther. In 1517 he published his 95 theses (i.e., complaints about the Catholic Church). As noted above, his complaints centered on the financial abuses by church leaders and on the Pope's jurisdiction over Purgatory (i.e., his authority to declare that anyone could simply pay money to reduce their time there or receive immediate release). Luther argued that the treasury of the Church was not dependent on the actions of the Saints (as the Catholic Church claimed), but on the Gospel itself. He insisted that the Bible was the only basis for making any kind of authoritative declaration, not the whim of a supposedly infallible Pope.

The underlying reasons that drove Luther to ultimately criticize the Catholic Church and its doctrine were as follows (Bainton et al., 2016). First, it was Luther's own struggle with sin. When reading the Bible, he became convinced that no amount of penance or good activity by humans was sufficient to atone for an inherently sinful nature that separated them from God. From this came Luther's belief that only by faith in the death and resurrection of Jesus Christ (justification by faith, not by works) could people be saved from hell (as emphasized by the apostle Paul in the New Testament). Based on his reading of Scripture, Luther believed that no one was worthy of salvation. Good works could not save a person, but were the natural result that flowed from the immense gratitude resulting from being saved and loved by God despite their irredeemable sinfulness.

Luther opposed Catholic Church doctrine in a number of other ways as well. In *The Babylonian Captivity of the Church*, Luther argued that the number of Catholic Sacraments should be decreased from seven to two (baptism and the Eucharist only) based on what Jesus Christ had implemented according to Scripture. Luther even denied the sacred Catholic doctrine of transubstantiation with regard to the Eucharist and instead argued that it be replaced by the doctrine of consubstantiation -- see below). This claim threatened the identity of the priest as the primary intercessor between people and God, thus challenging the hierarchical leadership of the Church and the Pope. Instead, Luther argued that according to Scripture, anyone with faith in Jesus Christ could approach God directly and didn't need the priest to intercede for them (i.e., the "priesthood of all believers"). As a result of these criticisms, Luther was declared by the Church to be a heretic of the first degree and should have been excommunicated and then executed (if it had not been for other circumstances -- see Marty's discussion in Bainton et al., which go beyond the scope of this brief review).

Luther soon began conversations with the German Catholic emperor Charles V, encouraging him to take back political power from the Church by opposing some of its doctrines. In 1529, the emperor and prominent German laypersons "protested" (and later rescinded) a ruling of the Church called the Diet of Speyer. "Protestant" was the name given to members of this moment who opposed the Catholic hierarchy and later to all those who rejected the rule of the Catholic Church during the Reformation.

In Switzerland, from the teachings of Huldrych Zwingli, a radical form of the Reformation emerged that argued for the separation of church and state and for making church membership voluntary, not compulsory (as it was in that day). Out of this movement came the Baptists, also called Anabaptists by critics because they denied the validity of infant baptism. The Baptists argued that baptism should occur only after individuals had reached the age of reason when they could decide for themselves whether or not to become a follower of Jesus Christ. It was from this tradition that the Mennonites, the Hutterites, the Amish, and the Quakers would later emerge.

Among other reformers of this period was John Calvin (1509-1564), who also emphasized the authority of Scripture and the universal nature of the church (not limited to Catholics but to all believing Christians), rejected the statues and images of holy persons (including the crucifix, except for a plain cross), and especially, argued for the doctrine of *predestination*, i.e., that only certain individuals ("the elect") were destined for heaven (vs. human free will). In order to determine who exactly the elect were (which no one could know for certain), Calvin said there were three tests: profession of faith in Jesus Christ, a disciplined Christian life, and love for the sacraments (particularly the Eucharist). Having passed these tests, one could rest assured that they were a member of the elect. Calvin's teachings would later lead to the Reformed traditions in Europe, from which the Presbyterian denomination would later emerge from the influence and leadership of John Knox of Scotland.

While the Lutheran and Reformed traditions were developing on the continent of Europe and northern British Isles, the Church of England under the leadership of King Henry VIII split off from the Catholic Church. This was not so much for religious reasons as for political ones. The King had a dispute with the Pope over his proposed marriage. Much of the Catholic doctrine, then, was retained by the King in this new movement that was to become the Anglican and Episcopal traditions. Several changes, however, were made. The King introduced the Bible written in common English into churches so that all had access to Scripture, removed all monasteries from England, and allowed clergy to marry. The doctrine of the new Church of England was described in the *Book of Common Prayer* (the Anglican counterpart to the *Catechism of the Catholic Church*).

Later, in the mid-18th century, Methodism branched off from the Anglican Church in England. The name "Methodism" was derived from the methodical study and devotion of its adherents. Led by the Oxford scholar John Wesley, this movement emphasized conversion to Christianity through evangelistic outreach and preaching by laypersons ("free churchmanship"). Methodist doctrine stressed salvation by faith, God's grace, and the living of a moral life as a follower of Jesus Christ. The movement spread rapidly in the rural areas of England, and soon came to Switzerland and the American colonies (particularly New York).

The Restoration movement also emerged around this time in the American colonies. The "Great Awakening" was in part a reaction to the growing scientific rationalism in England and Europe and in part a reaction to the formal expression of religious practice in traditional churches that lacked emotion and zeal. "Revivals" began to occur in many Protestant groups, particularly among Congregationalists, Presbyterians, and Baptists. Leaders of this movement included Jonathan Edwards and George Whitfield, whose fiery preaching and evangelistic style were particularly successful in converting those on the American frontier and later the un-churched in rapidly growing industrial centers.

The 19th century would see the rise of many new religious groups in America, as well as the growth of conservative, fundamentalist, and evangelical forms of Protestantism through revivals led by preachers such as Charles Spurgeon, Charles Finney, Dwight Moody, and William Booth (founder of the Salvation Army). The new forms of Protestantism that developed focused on individual conversion, commitment, and emotional forms of worship. Less emphasis was placed on church organization (characteristic of the mainline traditions). This period is also when a number of new non-traditional Christian Protestant groups emerged from the teachings of Joseph Smith (Mormons), Mary Baker Eddy (Christian Scientists), and Charles Taze Russell (Jehovah's Witnesses). The mid to late 19th century also saw the emergence of Seventh Day Adventists, a conservative Christian denomination that emphasized health and healing through a healthy diet and devout lifestyle. Under the leadership of Ellen White and her husband James White, the SDA church grew rapidly. Today, the Adventist Health System is the largest non-profit Protestant healthcare system in the U.S. (Byrd, 2016), second only to Catholic Healthcare.

Finally, the 20th century would see two World Wars between Christian countries and a Holocaust that greatly weakened Christendom in Europe, leading to rapid secularization and the growth of Communism and atheism. However, in the United States, the early 20th century (1901-1906) saw the rise of Pentecostal and Holiness movements that branched off from the Methodist tradition. This movement grew rapidly in the inner cities and among the rural poor in the South, and included charismatic practices such as "speaking in tongues" (glossolalia), "prophecy" (knowledge about a person that was divinely communicated), baptism in the Holy Spirit ("second baptism"), and belief in miraculous healings. The movement spread rapidly both in the U.S. and around the world (especially Latin America, the Caribbean, and Africa). By the 1960's, it had begun to influence mainline Protestant traditions, finding its way into Episcopalian, Lutheran, and Presbyterian congregations, and even Roman Catholic groups. Middle-class and well-educated congregations were now starting to get involved. Pentecostals and Charismatics today make up more than one-quarter of the world's Christians and the majority of Protestants (Pew Research Center, 2011).

As a reaction to scientific rationalism (particularly Darwin's theory of evolution) and the growth of liberal Protestant theology, Fundamentalism came into being in America with publication of *The Fundamentals* between 1910 and 1915, which maintained that the Bible was inerrant and should be taken literally (especially the Creation story). Leaders of this movement were William Jennings Bryan, and later, Jerry Falwell and Pat Robertson, who argued for the outlawing of abortion, the reintroduction of prayer in schools, the growth of the military, and support for Israel. Many of these views have also been adopted by Pentecostal and Charismatic groups.

More recently, Evangelicalism has arisen as a trans-denominational Protestant movement in the U.S. and around the world. Evangelical Protestantism was initiated by preachers such as Billy Graham, and has been supported by popular magazines such as *Christianity Today* and *Charisma*. Evangelicals focus on sharing the Christian message and conversion to a conservative form of Christianity based on the Bible (being "born again"). As mainline Protestant traditions (Methodist, Episcopal, Presbyterian) decline in numbers around the United States and the world, the number of Evangelicals is increasing. The U.S. now has more Evangelical Protestants than any other country in the world (Pew Research Center, 2011, p 46).

Admittedly, the review above has been a superficial overview of a very complex history of how the many Protestant traditions have come into being during the past 500 years. Nevertheless, it provides some sense of origin for the beliefs and practices that are common to many Protestants today. Those beliefs and practices have the potential to influence mental health.

CHAPTER 3

CORE PROTESTANT BELIEFS

Of course, with over 30,000 denominations, it is difficult to summarize the beliefs of all Protestants. However, most Protestants like Catholics accept the Nicene Creed as the core of their beliefs (**Table 1**). The only exceptions are non-traditional Christians and perhaps other smaller groups who reject the traditional creeds. In addition, many beliefs of Protestants are similar to those of Roman Catholics, from whom they split off as described earlier. Therefore, one way to summarize Protestant beliefs is to simply describe how these vary from Catholic beliefs. This approach is consistent with the cheeky claim by some that the only distinguishing feature of Protestants is that they are not Catholic. Indeed, the differences between Protestants and Catholics are truly minor, at least when compared to what non-Christian religions in the world belief. In fact, there has even been a growing movement to bring Catholics and Protestants back together, at least in terms of acknowledging their similarities and joining efforts to promote their common values (Ankerberg, & Weldon, 2012). Having acknowledged this ecumenical effort, however, here are differences in belief that separate the two groups that I will now describe.

Since there is no authoritative text for all Protestants, such as the *Catechism of the Catholic Church* for Catholics, and most sources favor either one group or the other, it is difficult to find credible sources that describe these differences with some sense of balance. Thus, the differences described here are summarized from several relatively recent sources that are more or less credible (Rasario, 2014; Lindberg et al., 2016; Nelson et al., 2016; Diffen, 2017), along with some additions and editorializing by the author (with his own biases). Generalizing anything about Protestant beliefs is fraught with danger, though, given the 30,000+ Protestant denominations, each of which believes something slightly different.

Ecclesiastical Authority

The Catholic faithful are guided and directed by the "magisterium," i.e., the house of cardinals and the Pope (considered infallible) who interpret Holy Scripture and church doctrine and make official pronouncements regarding doctrine and practice for contemporary application. Protestants as a group, and most individual denominations with some exceptions, have nothing similar to the Catholic hierarchical structure and leadership body. Instead, most Protestants believe in the "priesthood of all believers" such that every individual can develop an individual personal relationship with Jesus Christ and worship God, with or without intervening clergy. Protestants do not believe that there is anyone besides Jesus that is infallible (including the Pope). Furthermore, Protestants maintain that people can confess their sins to each other, rather than needing to confess them to a priest (based on James 5:16). However, some Protestant denominations (such as Anglicans, Methodists, Presbyterians, etc.) have retained a degree of hierarchical structure with priests, bishops and archbishops. For example, the Episcopal Church has an Executive Council that convenes a General Convention every three years and has bishops that oversee dioceses, similar to what Catholics have.

Table 1. The Nicene Creed [1]

We believe in one God, the Father, the Almighty, maker of heaven and earth, of all that is seen and unseen.

We believe in one Lord, Jesus Christ, the only Son of God, eternally begotten of the Father, God from God, Light from Light, true God from true God, begotten, not made, one in Being with the Father.

Through him all things were made. For us men and for our salvation he came down from heaven: by the power of the Holy Spirit he was born of the Virgin Mary, and became man.

For our sake he was crucified under Pontius Pilate; he suffered, died, and was buried.

On the third day he rose again in fulfillment of the Scriptures; he ascended into heaven and is seated on the right hand of the Father.

He will come again in glory to judge the living and the dead, and his kingdom will have no end.

We believe in the Holy Spirit, the Lord, the giver of life, who proceeds from the Father and the Son. With the Father and the Son he is worshipped and glorified. He has spoken through the Prophets.

We believe in one holy catholic and apostolic Church.

We acknowledge one baptism for the forgiveness of sins.

We look for the resurrection of the dead, and the life of the world to come. Amen.

---

[1] Nicene Creed. *Encyclopædia Britannica.* Retrieved on from https://www.britannica.com/topic/Nicene-Creed (accessed on 1/18/17)

Tradition

Protestants view tradition differently than do Catholics. While Catholics give equal value to Catholic Church history/tradition and Holy Scripture, Protestants use Scripture as the primary and for some, only source of authority. Tradition is viewed as a secondary source of authority, since God reveals himself through prayer and Scripture to individuals. In contrast, the Catechism of the Catholic Church states: "*Sacred Scripture* is the speech of God as it is put down in writing under the breath of the Holy Spirit. And [Holy] *Tradition* transmits in its entirety the Word of God which has been entrusted to the apostles by Christ the Lord and the Holy Spirit. It transmits it to the successors of the apostles so that, enlightened by the Spirit of truth, they may faithfully preserve, expound and spread it abroad by their preaching. As a result the Church, to whom the transmission and interpretation of Revelation is entrusted, 'does not derive her certainty about all revealed truths from the holy Scriptures alone. Both Scripture and Tradition must be accepted and honored with equal sentiments of devotion and reverence'" (Catholic Catechism, Part 1, Section 1, Chapter 2: 81-82). Thus, Catholics believe in sacred tradition that involves teachings from Jesus, the Apostles, early "Church fathers," and councils of Church leaders who help to interpret and clarify the Scriptures for their application in the world today. Protestants reject this notion. Most Protestants believe that Scripture is sufficient in itself (*Sola Scriptura*).

The Bible and Interpretation of Scripture

The Protestant Bible contains 39 books of the Hebrew Bible and 27 books of the New Testament, but not the seven additional books of the Hebrew Bible that the Catholic tradition includes (i.e., the *Apocrypha*) or the ten additional books that the Orthodox tradition includes. All traditions, however, agree on the 27 books of the New Testament. Protestants rely on the Bible as the authoritative source for all teachings and doctrines. With regard to interpretation of Scripture, there is great variation among Protestants, depending on where they fall on the conservative to liberal/progressive spectrum. Many of those on the conservative end believe that what is contained in the Bible is exactly what happened - the actual word of God without error (as Muslims believe about the Qur'an). At a minimum, Protestants rely on and interpret Scripture more literally than

Catholics, who at least historically have depended more on Catholic leaders (local priests, etc.) to interpret the Scripture for them.

Salvation and Sanctification

Salvation is another area where Protestants and Catholics differ. Based on the teachings of Martin Luther, many Protestants believe that salvation is by faith alone (*per solam fidem*), through grace alone (*sola gratia*), in Christ alone (*solus Christus*) (Ephesians 2:8-9). In many Protestant traditions, salvation occurs at a specific point when a person decides to surrender their life to Jesus Christ. This is particularly true for those on the conservative end of the spectrum, who believe that this is essential for salvation based on Romans 10:9-10. There is debate, however, about whether this act results in permanent, lifelong salvation (eternal security or "once saved, always saved" argument), or whether one can lose their salvation due to their sinful actions. Catholics, in contrast, see salvation as a process through which participating in the Catholic Church over time provides saving grace. In other words, Catholics believe that human activity ("works") plays an important role in the salvation process, whereas Protestants believe that people cannot earn their way to heaven but depend on faith in the death and resurrection of Jesus Christ. Rather than being a way to earn one's salvation, good works are the result of it. For Protestants, *sanctification* is the process after salvation that involves a person slowly conforming life to the teachings and example of Jesus Christ. Protestants vary in their beliefs about the role that free will plays in salvation, ranging from salvation being predetermined by God to salvation being determined by the free will of the individual.

The Eucharist or Communion

Protestants emphasize the holiness and sacredness of participating in communion. However, unlike Catholic and Orthodox believers, they do not believe that during the blessing of the elements that a miracle occurs where the wafer or host actually becomes the body of Christ and the wine (or grape juice) becomes the actual blood of Christ (transubstantiation). There is a belief among some Protestants, particularly Lutherans, that rather than literally becoming the body and blood of Christ, the elements remain what they are but that Jesus is present spiritually in and around them (consubstantiation). Other

Protestants on the conservative end of the spectrum view communion more symbolically, performed in memory of what Jesus Christ has done on the cross (without the communion elements being affected during the ritual).

Sin

Protestants and Catholics also differ in their view of sin. While Protestants believe that all sin is generally bad, Catholics place different grades on the severity of sin. Catholics believe there are venial sins (lesser sins that do not eternally separate a person from God) and mortal sins (greater sins that do). Catholics believe that mortal sins, when committed by a responsible person who knowingly does so through freedom of choice, separate a person eternally from God unless confessed and forgiven before death (the choice of words here is very important). This belief applies to those who commit suicide and cannot repent of this mortal sin, although Catholic teachings today emphasize that in order to commit a mortal sin, one must act without mental illness. Protestants, in contrast, believe that all sin involves disobeying God and has the potential to separate a person from God, and therefore should be avoided or repented of.

The Saints and Mary

Catholics *venerate* a number of designated Saints and Mary the mother of Jesus (they do not pray to them but rather pray *through* them). Catholics believe these individuals deserve veneration because of the holy lives they lived, and therefore may have special influence with God. Protestants (particularly those on the conservative end of the spectrum) believe that all persons who believe in Jesus Christ as their personal savior are Saints. They do not venerate Mary or pray through her or through the Saints. Protestants believe that they can go directly to God through Jesus Christ to request mercy, forgiveness, or favors. No intermediaries are needed, whether that involves Mary, Saints, angels, or a priest. In addition, Catholics believe that Mary like Jesus was also sinless, i.e., that Mary was "preserved from all stain of original sin" during her life (*Catechism of the Catholic Church*, Part 1, Section 2, Chapter 1:411). Protestants (and Orthodox Christians) believe that only Jesus was sinless.

The Rapture and Purgatory
Some evangelical and fundamentalist Protestants believe that *prior to* the Second Coming of Jesus Christ at the end of time, there will be seven years of difficult times and great suffering here on earth called the Great Tribulation (based on Daniel 9:27). They believe that Christians who are saved and alive at that time will be taken up into heaven before the Great Tribulation takes place. This is called the Rapture. Individuals who are raptured will be spared the suffering and physical death that all others will be subject to. Catholics, while they believe in the Second Coming of Jesus Christ when all the faithful will be taken up into heaven and reunited with Jesus/God (based on 1st Thessalonians 4:16-17), do not believe in a rapture.

With regard to Purgatory, Catholics believe that everyone must go here prior to entering heaven in order to be purified of their sins and be prepared to spend eternity with God. Protestants, in contrast, do not believe in such a state. After death, Protestants believe that people go either directly to heaven or, if they reject God, go directly to hell.

Infant Baptism
Many Protestant denominations (particularly those on the conservative, fundamentalist, and evangelical end of the spectrum) do not believe in infant baptism, but rather baptize members into the Christian faith only after they have reached an age of accountability. This is when an informed commitment is made on whether or not to accept Jesus Christ as Savior and Lord (called "believer's baptism"). However, other Protestants -- including Eastern Orthodox, Oriental Orthodox, Lutherans, Presbyterians, Methodists, Moravians, Anglicans and Episcopalians -- practice infant baptism like Catholics, although typically require "confirmation" once the individual has reached an age of accountability when the person makes a conscious commitment to the Christian faith (as Catholics do). Regardless, almost all Protestant denominations believe in at least a "blessing" ceremony during infancy that takes place in front of the congregation, where parents and other church members pledge to raise and guide the infant as they grow up in the Christian life.

Clergy and Worship Style

The clergy in Protestant denominations are typically called pastors, elders and deacons. Unlike Catholic priests who are appointed, required to be male and celibate, Protestant denominations may or may not officially "appoint" clergy (more likely among Mainline Protestants), typically allow clergy to marry and have families, and often allow women to be pastors and congregational leaders. Although there are celibate women clergy in the Catholic Church (called sisters or nuns), they cannot lead church services or celebrate the Mass. Some Protestant denominations such as Lutherans also have "deaconesses" who serve a similar role as Catholic sisters.

In contrast to Catholics, whose worship follows a relatively strict pattern and sequence of rituals that comprise the Mass, Protestants have a wide range of worship styles that may be formal (as in Episcopalian and Anglican traditions) or informal (as in Pentecostal and some Evangelical or Fundamentalist traditions). Days for worship also differ. While Catholics have many "holy days," most Protestants typically designate only Christmas and Easter as holy days (see Protestant Practices in the next chapter). Both Catholics and Protestants typically worship on Sundays (except for Seventh Day Adventists who worship on Saturday). While Catholics emphasize participation in the life of the Church through the sacraments, Protestants emphasize the Bible, prayer, communal worship, and fellowship. In contrast to Catholics, Protestants (especially conservative Protestants) typically do not have statues in their churches or homes, since this is believed to be a form of idolatry. Protestants believe such practices contradict the 2nd Commandment that says: "Thou shalt not make unto thee any graven image, or any likeness of any thing that is in heaven above, or that is in the earth beneath..." (Exodus 20:4-6).

Beliefs in Common with Catholics

While differences between the beliefs and practices of Protestants and Catholics (and to some extent Orthodox Christians) are many, these are dwarfed in comparison to the many similarities that unite these faith traditions. The Nicene Creed as noted earlier summarizes the beliefs that are common to most Christian traditions. Similarly, belief in Heaven and Hell is common, although notions about these places/states may differ among Protestants. An example of the many similarities (and differences) in belief between Protestants and Catholics is illustrated by a table of comparisons (see Diffen 2017). Both Protestants and Catholics distinguish themselves from other religions (Oriental religions and Dharmic religions. However, although Catholics and Protestants on the more liberal/progressive end of the spectrum have been increasingly ecumenical and accepting of other non-Christian religions.

CHAPTER 4

PROTESTANT PRACTICES

The beliefs above are given expression through Protestant practices, which vary as widely as do Protestant beliefs.

Attending Religious Services
Attending religious service regularly is encouraged, but not required by most Protestant denominations (and weekly attendance is not obligatory, as among Catholics). One reason for this is that there is no biblical basis for gathering together for worship at a particular frequency. However, Hebrews 10:25 does encourage regular meetings and warns those who are now involved in the religious community: "Not forsaking the assembling of ourselves together, as the manner of some is; but exhorting one another: and so much the more, as ye see the day approaching." This passage is often used by Protestant clergy to encourage regular (including weekly) attendance at religious services. According to the most recent Pew Research Center (2014a) survey, Jehovah's Witnesses are most likely to attend at least once/week (85%), followed by Mormons (77%), Evangelical Protestants (58%), Historically Black Protestants (53%), and Mainline Protestants (33%), compared to Catholics (39%) and Eastern Orthodox (31%).

Prayer

Protestants believe in prayer as a way of enhancing one's relationship with God, and so strongly encourage it. Other reasons are that Jesus prayed regularly (Mark 1:35; Luke 5:16) and encouraged his followers to do likewise (Matthew 6:7-13; Matthew 7:11), and prayer is emphasized throughout both the New Testament (Philippians 4:6; Hebrews 4:15) and the Old Testament (Jeremiah 33:3; 2 Chronicles 7:14). In fact, the Scriptures stress that Christians should "pray without ceasing" (1 Thessalonians 5:17). The prevalence of daily or more frequent prayer varies depending on denomination in the U.S.: Evangelical Protestants (79%), Historically Black Protestants (80%), Mainline Protestants (54%), Orthodox Christians (57%), and Catholics (59%) (Pew Research Center, 2014b).

Bible Reading

Because of the importance of the Bible to Protestant Christians (vs. church tradition among Catholics), Bible reading is strongly encouraged. Those who read the Bible weekly or more often) are Jehovah's Witnesses (88%), Mormons (77%), Evangelical Protestants (63%), and Historically Black Protestants (61%). This contrasts with Mainline Protestants (30%), Orthodox Christians (29%), and Catholics (25%) (Pew Research Center, 2014c).

Donating Money or Time

In many conservative and fundamentalist Protestant denominations, members are asked to "tithe" 10% of their gross annual income to the church. According to the Philanthropy Roundtable, Catholics give on average 1.5% of their gross income; Mainline Protestants give 2.9%; and Evangelical and Charismatic or Pentecostal Christians such as the Assemblies of God give 4% to 8% (Dunn, 2001). A national U.S. survey the Gallup Poll in 2013 reported that Protestant Christians (85%) were more likely to donate money than Catholics (79%) or those with no religious affiliation (77%) (Gallup Poll, 2013). With regard to donating time, Protestants are also more likely to have volunteered (for religious or other organizations) in the past 12 months (69%) compared to Catholics (57%) or those with no religious affiliation (53%) (Gallup Poll, 2013).

Fasting

The frequency, length, and type of fasting various widely across religious groups in Christianity. Greek Orthodox Christians fast 180-200 days each year, including the Nativity Fast (40 days before Christmas), Lent (48 days before Easter), and Assumption (15 days in August). Fasting is optional for most Protestants (i.e., not obligatory as with Catholics or Eastern Orthodox), although individual fasting is encouraged. Evangelical Protestants are more likely to fast than mainline Protestants (Beliefnet, 2001). A popular fast among Evangelical Protestants is the Daniel Fast (based on Daniel 1:8-14). This involves eating nothing but vegetables (pulse) and water for 10 days (Trepanowski & Bloomer, 2010).

Observing Holy Days

As noted earlier, Protestant Christians are less likely to emphasize specific Holy Days than Catholics or Eastern Orthodox Christians, and instead emphasize that each day is holy and should be celebrated as such. According to Psalm 118:24, "This is the day which the LORD hath made; we will rejoice and be glad in it." Thus, one day or the other does not merit any special reverence over other days. However, almost all Protestants celebrate Christmas, Good Friday, and Easter, and may have special religious services on these days. Depending on the particular Protestant denomination, other days and seasons of the year may be important including Advent, Epiphany (commemorating the visit of the Magi to the Christ child), Lent (Ash Wednesday or the entire five weeks before Easter), Holy Week (the week before Easter, especially Palm Sunday, Maundy Thursday, and Good Friday), Pentecost (7th Sunday after Easter when the Holy Spirit descended on Christ's disciples), Ascension Day (when Jesus ascended into heaven), and All Saints Day.

Baptism

As noted earlier, baptism may be performed as either an infant or as an adult after the person has reached the age of accountability. However, most Protestant denominations baptize members to initiate them into the denomination. Some of the more conservative, fundamentalist or charismatic denominations may in addition encourage a Baptism of the Holy Spirit, where the individual may "speak in tongues" and receive the gift of the Holy Spirit, which gives them the power and boldness to testify to their faith.

Confirmation

Protestant denominations that practice infant Baptism usually require a ceremony where the person confirms their belief and makes a public commitment to the teachings of the faith. This is called confirmation, and is similar to that which Catholics undergo during their early teen years. Receiving the Baptism of the Holy Spirit for some Protestant denominations may also serve as a kind of confirmation. Regardless, whatever name is given to this practice, it involves equipping the person with the *gifts* of the Holy Spirit to be used in serving God. These gifts are listed in at least three places in the New Testament and have considerable overlap. In 1 Corinthians 12:28-30, the gifts are listed as leadership positions (apostles, prophets, and teachers), ability to perform miracles and healing, ability to helping others, and the gift of serving in church administration. In 1 Corinthians 12:7-10 the gifts of the Holy Spirit are listed as ability to receive messages of wisdom or knowledge, the gift of faith, gifts of healing and miracles, gifts of prophecy, tongues or interpretations, and the ability to distinguish between spirits. Finally, Romans 12:6-8 describes the gifts of the Holy Spirit as prophesying, serving, teaching, encouraging, giving to others, leading others, and showing mercy. These gifts of the Holy Spirit must be distinguished from those conferred to Catholics during confirmation (wisdom, understanding, right judgment, courage, knowledge, reverence, and wonder or awe), and are also different from the *fruit* of the Holy Spirit which include love, joy, peace, forbearance, kindness, goodness, faithfulness, gentleness and self-control (Galatians 5:16).

Eucharist

For most Protestant Christians, the Eucharist (also called Holy Communion) is an important practice that usually takes place in church and involves receiving the wafer (body of Christ) and drinking the wine or grape juice (blood of Christ). Communion practices, though, may vary between denominations. Any believer is usually eligible to participate in the Eucharist ceremony, although some denominations may have certain regulations. As noted earlier, Protestants view receiving the Eucharist as an expression of faith, obedience to Christ, as a remembrance of Christ's death on the cross of human sins, and as a time of renewal of personal commitment.

Penance (confession)
Most Protestants do not believe in confessing one's sins to clergy, but rather follow the biblical injunction to confess one's sins to one another (based on James 5:16) or go directly to God (Matthew 6:12). However, Anglicans, Lutherans, and Methodists engage in group confession during religious services, and in select cases, may also engage in private confession to their clergy, with the clergy providing absolution. Again, this practice varies widely, and most members of conservative or fundamentalist traditions do not confess their sins to clergy, but rather to God or to one another.

Matrimony
Although Protestants do not consider marriage a sacrament (as do Catholics and Eastern Orthodox Christians), they do consider it sacred, holy, and the most intimate of human relationships. Marriage is not a temporary contract, but rather a life-long commitment. Divorce is highly discouraged among Protestants, based on Matthew 19:2-6, but is not considered a "mortal sin" as it is in Catholicism. Divorce rates are higher among Conservative Protestants than other religious groups, although there are many reasons for this, non-religious factors in particular (lower education, earlier age of marriage, earlier age of parenthood, and lower income) (Glass & Levchak, 2014).

Miscellaneous Practices
Other common religious practices of Protestants include listening to religious music, watching religious programs on television, reading inspirational Christian books (besides the Bible), wearing a cross on a necklace (simple cross, not a crucifix with Jesus on it, like some Catholics may wear), and for more evangelical traditions, placing a "fish" sign on their automobiles. "Witnessing" to others (sharing the Gospel) may also be very important for some Evangelical Christians, since failure to do so may have consequences in the hereafter based on Ezekiel 3:17-18, Ezekiel 33:6-9, and Acts 18:5-6 (the other person's "blood will be on their hands"). Mental health professionals need to be aware of such beliefs, since patients may seek to evangelize or share their faith with them for this reason; understanding and toleration can go a long way.

CHAPTER 5

PROTESTANT VALUES

Protestant ethics and values reflect their beliefs and practices. The values held by Protestants are similar to those held by Catholics, although Protestants on the more conservative end of the spectrum have values that are probably more like Catholics then do Protestants on the progressive end. These values include belief in the sanctity of human life, respect for human dignity, respect for creation, attitudes towards helping the poor and less fortunate, efforts to correct social injustices, emphasis on justice, compassion, forgiveness, peace, faithfulness, honesty and integrity, and the importance of hard work and independence. I now discuss each of these below.

Respect for Human Life
Most Protestant Christians believe that men and women are created in God's image. Therefore, human life is considered precious and sacred, whether a person is young, old, healthy, sick, or disabled. From this belief comes mainline and conservative Protestant teachings concerning abortion, physician-assisted suicide/ euthanasia, suicide, and the death penalty.

    Abortion. The Protestant values regarding abortion will differ depending on the particular beliefs concerning the balance of views towards women's rights (advocated by more progressive Protestant traditions) and views toward preserving life at all cost (advocated by Conservative or Evangelical Protestant traditions). The right of women over their own bodies is as strongly held by some Protestants as the right to life is held by other Protestants. Some Mainline, many Conservative, and most Fundamentalist and Evangelical traditions now support abortion only in cases where the mother's life is in danger (or for some, in cases of rape). These Protestants defend their views based on Biblical scriptures, a few which follow here:

"Before I formed you in the womb I knew you; before you came to birth I consecrated you" (Jeremiah 1:5)

"My frame was not hidden from you, when I was being made in secret, intricately wrought in the depths of the earth" (Psalm 22:10-11)

"For so many marvels I thank you; a wonder am I, and all your works are wonders. You knew me through and through, my being held no secrets from you, when I was being formed in secret, textured in the depths of the earth. Your eyes could see my embryo. In your book all my days were inscribed, every one that was fixed is there" (Psalm 139:14-16).

Physician-Assisted Suicide or Euthanasia. Most Protestant Christians believe in the 6th commandment, "Thou shalt not kill" (Exodus 20:13), and maintain that those who are weak, sick, or whose cognitive state has been adversely affected by illness still have a right to life, which only God has the power to end. Sometimes efforts to relieve suffering may end up causing death, but the intention should never be to cause death. On the other hand, some progressive Protestants may believe that assisted suicide may be ethical in special cases where suffering is severe and cannot be relieved.

Suicide. The commandment "Thou shalt not kill" also applies to killing oneself. However, Protestant Christians may be more lenient than Catholic Christians in this regard. Emile Durkheim, the founder of modern sociology, observed in 1897 that suicide was more common in Protestants than Catholics, arguing that there was greater "social control" and social integration among Catholics than

Protestants. Recent findings appear to confirm these earlier reports, although emphasize the role that Catholic theology has played (see VanderWeele et al., 2016, and Koenig, 2016). Catholics for years (until recent times) believed that suicide was a "mortal sin" that eternally separate one from God and destined the person to spend eternity in hell. Most Protestants, in contrast, do not grade sins as Catholics do, and do they believe in mortal sins. These views may influence the suicide threshold in vulnerable individuals.

Death Penalty. Protestant Christians vary widely on their views concerning the death penalty. Those on the more conservative or fundamentalist end of the spectrum tend to favor it (despite strong belief in the sanctity of human life), more so than those on the progressive or liberal end of the spectrum. Issues related to justice, forgiveness, and potential for rehabilitation all come into play in deciding for or against this practice. Most Protestant or Catholic denominations oppose the death penalty in most cases, unless the crime is so heinous and the criminal so unrepentant that the person is unredeemable (most Christians, though, don't believe anyone is beyond the love of God). Protestants, like Catholics, believe that the punishment must be proportional to the crime committed, and the death penalty is only appropriate if the guilty party's identity and responsibility are fully determined.

Respect for Human Dignity

This value, related to respect for human life, includes the belief that all people are unique, have something to offer, and have infinite worth and value to their Creator. This leads to efforts to defend human rights whenever they are being violated, and is an especially important value among many Protestants who adhere to the "Social Gospel." In the 20th Century, a group of Protestant clergy sought to rid the world poverty, unequal civil rights, and other social evils by preaching a social gospel (see Rauschenbusch, 1917). However, Protestants vary widely in their views concerning how much effort should be made towards correcting social injustices, as opposed to converting unbelievers and spreading the gospel message. Progressive/liberal Protestant denominations are more likely to stress a social gospel, which means that efforts should not only be directed towards evangelism and conversion, but also toward social reform. In these traditions, social reform may be given priority over evangelism. This view is one of many reasons for categorizing Protestants as conservative, moderate, or progressive/liberal (which tend to follow political lines as well). Bear in mind, again, that these statements are generalizations that have many exceptions.

Responsibility for Creation
Many Protestants, particularly those on the progressive end of the spectrum, value the natural world's beauty and feel responsible for being a good steward of that beauty. Thus, they advocate for initiatives that preserve the environment for future generations, and promote concern for issues such as global warming, preservation of the natural environment though parks and recreation areas, and ensuring clean water and air. In the beginning, God put humans in charge of taking care of his amazing creation: "And God blessed them, and God said unto them, Be fruitful, and multiply, and replenish the earth, and subdue it: and have dominion over the fish of the sea, and over the fowl of the air, and over every living thing that moveth upon the earth" (Genesis 1:28)

Justice and Respect for the Law
Justice means respecting each other's rights with a desire to establishing harmony and equal treatment of all, including caring for those who are vulnerable. One source for these views is Leviticus 19:15: "Ye shall do no unrighteousness in judgment: thou shalt not respect the person of the poor, nor honor the person of the mighty: but in righteousness shalt thou judge thy neighbour." Justice includes obeying the laws of the land as established by the government: "Let every soul be subject unto the higher powers. For there is no power but of God: the powers that be are ordained of God. Whosoever therefore resisteth the power, resisteth the ordinance of God: and they that resist shall receive to themselves damnation" (Romans 13:1-2).

Love and Compassion
Protestant Christians value the second Great Commandment: "Thou shalt love thy neighbour as thyself" (Matthew 22:39). According to John 13:34-35, when Protestant Christians show love like this they let others know that they are followers of Jesus: "A new commandment I give unto you, That ye love one another; as I have loved you, that

ye also love one another. By this shall all men know that ye are my disciples, if ye have love one to another." Jesus goes further still by telling his disciples that they should also love their enemies and even those who hurt them (Luke 6:27-32). Showing respect, compassion, and sensitivity to the weak and needy is another way that Protestants show that they are followers of Jesus, and when they treat others in this way, the Bible says they are essentially caring for Jesus himself:

> "For I was hungry, and ye gave me meat: I was thirsty, and ye gave me drink: I was a stranger, and ye took me in: Naked, and ye clothed me: I was sick, and ye visited me: I was in prison, and ye came unto me. Then shall the righteous answer him, saying, Lord, when saw we thee hungry, and fed thee? or thirsty, and gave thee drink? When saw we thee a stranger, and took thee in? or naked, and clothed thee? Or when saw we thee sick, or in prison, and came unto thee? And the King shall answer and say unto them, Verily I say unto you, Inasmuch as ye have done it unto one of the least of these my brethren, ye have done it unto me" (Matthew 25:35-40).

Service

Because of the high value placed on compassion and love, Protestant Christians believe that they have been "called" by God to serve others. As faith-based organizations, many Protestant denominations (and individual local congregations) provide care for the hungry and the poor, run soup kitchens, operate shelters for the homeless, maintain clothing stores and food pantries, and respond when disasters strike communities in the U.S. and around the world. For a listing of organizations and services that Protestant faith-based groups provide, see two white papers (now books) produced for the White House Office of Faith-based Initiatives (Koenig, 2004; 2006).

Forgiveness

Protestant Christians believe in forgiveness of others because of what Jesus said in many places in the Gospels, but particularly in the Lord's Prayer: "forgive us our debts, as we have forgiven those who are in debt to us" (Mathew 6:12-15). Unless they forgive others, Protestant Christians believe that God will not forgive them. Protestants also believe that holding a grudge is incompatible with being one of his followers, as indicated in Matthew 5:21-24: "You have heard that it was said to those of old, 'You shall not murder; and whoever murders will be liable to judgment.' But I say to you that everyone who is angry with his brother will be liable to judgment; whoever insults his brother will be liable to the council; and whoever says, 'You fool!' will be liable to the hell of fire. So if you are offering your gift at the altar and there remember that your brother has something against you, leave your gift there before the altar and go. First be reconciled to your brother, and then come and offer your gift." The high value that Protestant Christians place on the Bible makes it hard to ignore these sacred passages voiced by the person whose name they are called by.

Peace

Jesus emphasizes that those who follow his teachings will experience peace: "These things I have spoken unto you, that in me ye might have peace" (John 16:33). He also refers to those who make peace with others as blessed: "Blessed are the peacemakers: for they shall be called the children of God" (Matthew 5:9). He is referred to as the "Prince of Peace" in Isaiah 9:6. Thus, anger and conflict are not condoned in the New Testament, except in rare instances to illustrate a point or to defend moral principles. For example, Jesus said "Think not that I am come to send peace on earth: I came not to send peace, but a sword. For I am come to set a man at variance against his father, and the daughter against her mother, and the daughter in law against her mother in law" (Matthew 10:34-36). This was said to remind his followers that they would be persecuted for their beliefs by others, sometimes even those in their own household. Jesus also "cursed" a fig tree (Matthew 21:18-22), which was an illustration of the Pharisees who were not producing fruit that was expected of them. He also got physically violent with those who were not respecting God's house (Matthew 21:12), representing a righteous type of anger necessary to oppose the manipulation of sacred places for self-gain. Thus, Protestant Christians believe that peace should be the rule, although there are exceptions.

Faithfulness

Protestants, like Catholics, value relationships that are based on trust and loyalty, especially when applied to marital fidelity, but also in relationships with other family members, friends, and co-workers more generally. As noted earlier, Protestants believe in the sanctity of marriage and do not condone adultery in any form (including pornography, based on Matthew 5:28). Being faithful means doing what one says one will do, i.e., being responsible for tasks that one is entrusted with. Protestants believe this includes being faithful in terms of serving the local church.

Honesty and Integrity
Finally, Protestant Christians value being truthful, not holding secrets that might harm other persons or relationships, and not saying hurtful things about others behind their backs. This applies to institutions as well as individuals, and is a value that flows naturally from the second Great Commandment, i.e., to love neighbor as self and to treat others as one wishes to be treated (see love and compassion above).

Work Ethic
Finally, much has been written about the "Protestant work ethic" that distinguishes this Protestant value from that of other faith groups (Furnham, 1984). The work ethic describes a philosophy of life that emphasizes hard work, self-discipline, and frugality. These are characteristics that many of those in the U.S. (which started out and remains largely Protestant) claim with pride and attribute their own and their nation's economic success to. Many Protestants hold these principles in high regard, along with being independent and self-sufficient. While considered a positive value in many cases, however, there are also situations (such as unemployment) when the Protestant ethic may be associated with poor mental health outcomes (Ezzy, 1993).

As noted earlier, Protestants and Catholics share these Christian values. Many of the values above, if practiced and held to, will impact mental and social health in a variety of ways. I now speculate on some of those ways in the next chapter.

CHAPTER 6

CHRISTIANITY AND MENTAL HEALTH: SPECULATIONS

In this chapter, I speculate on the impact that Protestant beliefs, practices, and values (BPVs) may have on mental health. As noted earlier, Protestant Christians believe in a personal God with whom they can relate and interact, who is loving, forgiving, merciful, and just, and desires that they should love one another as he loves them. These beliefs, and the practices and values that flow from them, should affect mental health, particularly during times of stress, adversity, and loss. The following comments on the hypothetical positive or negative effects of Protestant BPVs on mental health are based on psychological, behavioral, and social mechanisms. Since Protestants vary so widely on these BPVs, however, these comments are quite general and may depend on the particular branch of Protestantism.

Positive Effects
What are the positive effects that might results from deeply held Protestant Christian BPVs? "Deeply held" is an important qualifier here, since superficial or weakly held beliefs are unlikely to affect attitudes or behaviors to a sufficient degree that mental health would be impacted. This may also depend on how much support such

BPVs receive from the surrounding community, both the particular religious community and the broader community.

<u>Psychological</u>. Protestants focus on the Bible, particularly the New Testament. The New Testament Gospels emphasize reasons why God became a human in Jesus Christ. Besides dying for the sins of humanity and making salvation and eternal life possible, Jesus announces at the very beginning of his ministry why he came: "The Spirit of the Lord is upon me, because he hath anointed me to preach the gospel to the poor; he hath sent me to heal the brokenhearted, to preach deliverance to the captives, and recovering of sight to the blind, to set at liberty them that are bruised..." (Luke 4:18; see also John 8:36). Similarly, in the Sermon on the Mount, Jesus says: "Blessed are they that mourn: for they shall be comforted" (Matthew 5:4). He also says "The thief cometh not, but for to steal, and to kill, and to destroy: I am come that they might have life, and that they might have it more abundantly (John 10:10). Thus, the founder of the Christian faith says that the reason why he came was to heal the brokenhearted and bruised, bring comfort to those who mourn, set people free from their imprisonments, and enable people to live life abundantly. All of those reasons are related to good mental health. As a result, his followers should have more of it.

The doctrine of justification by faith, not works, and the immediate forgiveness of sins through belief and commitment to Jesus Christ, may also impact mental health. This applies especially to individuals dealing with emotional issues related to guilt and shame over past actions (addiction, substance abuse, crime and other antisocial behaviors). Feeling completely cleansed of sin and assured of heaven (as some Protestants believe salvation confers) should provide hope, optimism, and reassurance of life after death that is better than the one here on earth (freedom from all trial and suffering). Religious conversion among Protestant may be accompanied by discovery of new purpose and meaning that affects feelings about the self, other people, and motivates the person to engage in pro-social activities (volunteerism, honesty in business, emphasis on family responsibilities), all of which may enhance mental health, quality of social relationships, and well-being. Many Protestants believe that "Good News" (gospel) was that one had to be "born again," indicating that that everyone deserved a second chance, no matter what they had done, and indeed needed to go through such a transformative second birth.

Finally, given the important value that Protestants place on the Bible, the stories contained therein produce a framework that "name" what is going on inside the individual. These stories are archetypal, i.e., represent larger stories that apply to individual stories across time and generation. Consider the book of Job, the story about a person who loses everything, asks God "why," and then told by his closest friends that he must have sinned to explain his misfortune. This is the same story that many people with depression and grief have, and the reason why many come into counseling to address following loss and change. Such stories give meaning to life events and hope for a better day.

<u>Behavioral</u>. Protestant beliefs discourage alcohol intoxication, drug use, and other activities that harm the mind or the body (considered the "temple of the Holy Spirit" based on 1 Corinthians 6:19). The Protestant work ethic encourages hard work, diligence in school, frugality, honesty, and responsibility, all of which in most situations should lead to productivity and success in life. A productive life, in turn, should enhance self-esteem and reduce anxiety from poverty, lack, and dependence on others.

<u>Social</u>. Involvement in Protestant congregations may lead to greater social support, given the particular emphasis on fellowship and social interactions (more so than in Catholicism, which focuses more on the sacraments than on fellowship). Social interaction of this kind is often mutually supportive, involving the sharing of difficulties, challenges and trials ("confess yours sins to one another" based on James 5:16). Interactions with other church members may also lead to pro-social peer groups, in contrast to anti-social networks centered on drugs, alcohol, or criminal activity. The importance of marriage and fidelity within marriage among Protestants should lead to less divorce, more intact families, and positive rearing environments for children. This may be particularly important in later life when family support is needed as health fails (and when such support is lacking may lead to worse mental health).

Negative Effects

In contrast to positive benefits, how might Protestant BPVs adversely affect mental health? Again, psychological, behavioral, and social mechanisms are discussed.

Psychological. Protestants are commanded to hold to high standards with regard to attitude and conduct: put God first in your life (Mark 12:30), love your neighbor as yourself (Mark 12:31), love your enemy, bless those who curse you, do good to those who hate you, pray for those who use and persecute you (Matthew 5:44), forgive those who hurt you (Matthew 6:12), sell all you have and follow Jesus (Matthew 19:21), and so forth. Many Protestants as frail human beings may have difficulty living up to such lofty expectations based on their Holy Scriptures. This can result in psychological strains and feelings of guilt and shame for "not living up," especially for those who are psychologically vulnerable (Exline, 2002). The fire and brimstone preaching of some Protestant preachers (particularly those on the conservative or fundamentalist end of the spectrum) may create fear and anxiety in the faithful, as these often well-meaning faith leaders attempt to motivate non-believers to change attitudes and behavior for the better.

Failure to share their faith or "witness" to others about salvation in Jesus Christ may also cause guilt in some Evangelical Christians who feel that otherwise the non-saved individuals' "blood will be on their hands" (as noted above). This may arouse deep feelings of guilt and fear they will be responsible for the other's lack of salvation because they have not been witnessing. Likewise, impelled to ensure the salvation of others when nearing death – particularly close family members whom they perceive as not saved – the Evangelical Christian may try to coerce them on their deathbed into saying the prayer of salvation, believing that otherwise they will be lost forever and separated from them for eternity. This may create great distress in the person who is attempting to share their faith if resistance is encountered, in the person who is dying, and in other family members who are upset by this behavior. Mental health professionals should be alert to such possibilities when treating Christians with these views.

Finally, emphasis on the "prosperity gospel" and "divine healing" may cause emotional distress among those whose lives are not prospering or who are not healed from their diseases. Those individuals may be further burdened by members of their faith tradition who accuse them of having unconfessed sin in their lives (like Job's counselors did), say they lack sufficient faith, or claim that they are not applying themselves hard enough in prayer. If God rewards those who serve him diligently and heals the sick, how can one explain a person's poverty or failure to be healed? (other than by their lack of faith, sin, etc.) Such explanations are necessary in order to support this prosperity theology (and the promises in Scripture that adherents of this theology often point to). The burden is placed square onto the shoulders of the unfortunate poor person or the one who is sick.

<u>Behavioral</u>. Related to the prosperity gospel, some Protestant leaders may manipulate others for financial gain, promising health and wealth to those who turn over there money to them. Vulnerable individuals seeking approval may give beyond their means, leading to disappointment and even loss of faith when these promises are not fulfill. Likewise, those searching for acceptance and inclusion may join small Protestant sects that may force members to turn over all of their possessions and even break ties with family and community in order to prove their loyalty to the sect. The same applies to unscrupulous some charismatic preachers who are accountable to no one but themselves as they lead their sheep to the slaughter.

<u>Social</u>. Some Protestants believe their religion is the only true religion, and that others are destined for hell unless they convert and believe as they do. Having the "true religion" may fulfill certain ego and self-esteem needs, leading a "better than thou" attitude that raises them above those who believe differently. This may result in discrimination and condemnation of others, adversely affecting relationships within a community. Such beliefs may also create strife within the family, resulting in the ostracizing of members who lack the "correct" religious views.

A note of caution must be included here. People self-select themselves into various Protestant denominations, i.e., are free to choose whatever denomination they feel comfortable in and agrees with their personal beliefs. Therefore, one cannot conclude that Protestant denominations which adhere to a fundamentalist doctrine that "puts the fear of God" into its members is necessarily pathological or leads to worse mental health. Indeed, a study co-authored by a former president of the American Psychological Association (Martin E.P. Seligman) has found that Christian fundamentalists experienced significantly more positive emotions than members of more moderate or mainline Protestant traditions (Sethi & Seligman, 1993; 1994).

CHAPTER 7

CHRISTIANITY AND MENTAL HEALTH: THE RESEARCH

Research studies seldom include only Protestants, only Orthodox, or only Catholics. Since most of the research involving Christians comes from the United States and the United Kingdom, where the majority of the population is Protestant (51.5% and 54.5%, respectively) (Pew Research Center, 2011), the research findings on religiosity and mental health has been summarized below for Christians-majority populations. Given that strategy, the reader should be aware that these studies also include not only Protestant Christians but also a substantial number of Catholics (and some Eastern Orthodox as well).

The research findings presented here are based on a comprehensive and systematic review of the literature up through 2010 (Koenig et al., 2012) that focuses on Christians (Koenig & Al Shohaib, 2014, p 123). Since this literature summary is now rather dated, a few more recent studies are also described that illustrate more recent findings since that earlier review. A more comprehensive review of recent research from which these studies are taken is available elsewhere (CSTH, 2017). The present research review focuses on religious coping, depression, self-esteem, suicide, anxiety, ubstance use/abuse, psychosis, psychological well-being, locus of control, personality traits, and social health.

Religious Coping

Over 400 quantitative studies were conducted prior to 2010 that document a high prevalence of religious coping among Christians when facing psychological stressors, important losses, traumatic events, or changes in physical health. For example, one study of medically ill hospitalized patients found that 90% said they used religion to help them to cope with health problems, and over 40% indicated (spontaneously without prompting) that their religious belief was the most important factor that kept them going (Koenig, 1998). Likewise, in a national survey of the U.S. population after the September 11th terrorist attacks on the World Trade Centers reported in the *New England Journal of Medicine*, researchers found that 90% of respondents indicated they turned to religion as a primary way of coping with the anxiety and stress of this period (Schuster et al., 2001). Christian religious beliefs provide meaning to negative life circumstances, help to guide people on how to respond to negative life events, and provide a community of support that helps to counteract stress and prevent the negative emotions that often follow such stressors. Hundreds of additional qualitative studies have been published that verify these conclusions from quantitative studies. But is that really true? Is religious involvement related to better mental health and improved coping with stress?

Depression

There were 414 quantitative studies in Christian majority populations published up through 2010. Of those, 254 (61%) reported a significant inverse correlation between religiosity/spirituality (R/S) and depression. In contrast, 26 studies (6%) reported a significant positive relationship between R/S and depression. Inverse relationships between religiosity and depression appear to be particularly strong among those who are experiencing stressful life circumstances, suggesting a stress-buffering effect (Smith et al., 2003).

Among observational studies, particularly those with a cross-sectional designs, it is not possible to identify the direction of causation in the relationships identified, underscoring the need for prospective studies and clinical trials. Lower rates of depression among those who are more religious may simply mean that depression prevents religious involvement (rather than religion preventing depression). A more recent prospective study reported exactly that, i.e., those who were depressed were more likely over time to stop or reduce their attendance at religious services (Maselko et al., 2012). In contrast, a 12-year prospective study of 48,984 women (53% Protestant) participating in the Nurses' Health Study conducted by the Harvard School of Public Health found that effects were actually bidirectional in nature, i.e., religious attendance prevented depression and depression prevented religious attendance (Li et al., 2016). Results were similar when examined in Protestants and Catholics separately.

Of 28 randomized clinical trials (RCTs), 17 (61%) reported a significant reduction in depressive symptoms among those receiving a religious or spiritual (R/S) intervention greater than in those receiving standard care or a control condition; only two RCTs (7%) reported that R/S interventions were less effective. More recently, in a RCT that compared religious cognitive behavioral therapy (RCBT) to conventional secular CBT (CCBT) in 132 person with major depressive disorder (62% Protestant), both treatments decreased depressive significantly over time and to a similar degree. However, RCBT was particularly effective in highly religious clients, who also tended to be more compliant with RCBT than with CCBT (Koenig et al., 2015).

Self-Esteem
Research has also examined associations between religiosity and self-esteem, which tends to be low among those with depression. Of 65 studies in Christian majority samples published prior to 2010, 40 (62%) reported significantly great self-esteem in those who were more R/S and only two (3%) found lower self-esteem. These findings are consistent with those for depression.

Suicide
Prior to 2010, 126 studies had examined the relationship between religiosity and attitudes toward suicide, suicidal thoughts, or suicidal behaviors in Christian-majority populations. Of those studies, 99

(79%) found inverse or negative relationships and two (2%) reported positive relationships. In the one of the largest and most rigorous studies on suicide incidence to date, VanderWeele and colleagues (2016) from the Harvard School of Public Health analyzed data from a 14-year prospective study of 89,708 women (52% Protestant) participating in the Nurse's Health Study. They found that women attending religious services at least weekly were 84% less likely to commit suicide than women who never attended (hazard ratio=0.16, 95% CI=0.06-0.46), with more than a five-fold reduction in suicide incidence rate from 7 per 100,000 person-years to only 1 per 100,000 person-years. Results were similar when excluding women who were depressed or had chronic illness at baseline. When analyses were stratified by denomination, the risk among Catholics attending once per week or more was 95% lower compared to those attending less often (HR=0.05, 95% CI, 0.006-0.48). The risk, however, was approximately seven times lower in Catholics than in Protestants (HR 0.34, 95% CI=0.10-1.10). The greater effect in Catholics was explained by the strong prohibitions against suicide (with threat of eternal damnation, which many Catholics still associate with suicide), compared to more lenient attitudes toward suicide among Protestants.

Anxiety

Of 245 studies that explored relationships between R/S and anxiety in Christians, 120 (49%) reported inverse relationships between R/S and anxiety, whereas 24 (10%) found positive relationships. Almost all of these studies were cross-sectional, again limiting speculations on whether religious involvement was the primary factor explaining the relationship or whether anxiety was the primary factor. While religious beliefs can promote anxiety by instilling guilt and fear of eternal damnation, anxiety is also a powerful motivator for religious practice ("there are no atheists in foxholes"). There is another old adage that says "religion comforts the afflicted and afflicts the comforted," suggesting a bidirectional effect may be present as with depression. Of 26 RCTs in Christian populations that included various forms of meditation or other religious interventions, 16 (62%) reported a reduction in anxiety, one reported an increase in anxiety (4%), eight reported no effect (31%), and one reported both positive and negative effects.

Substance Use/Abuse

Of 260 studies that examined R/S and alcohol use/abuse in Christians, 233 (87%) reported significant inverse relationships. Only 4 studies (1.5%) reported positive relationships between R/S and greater alcohol use/abuse. Of 182 studies that focused on R/S and illicit drug use/abuse, 154 (85%) found significant inverse relationships and only two (1%) found positive relationships. More recently, Good and Willoughby (2011) analyzed data on 3,993 adolescents surveyed three to four times between 2003 and 2008. Religious affiliations of the geographical region where the study took place were 37% Catholic and 42% Protestant. Religious service attendance and non-religious activity (attendance at clubs at school and outside of school) were assessed. Substance use included frequency of alcohol use, amount of alcohol used per drinking episode, cigarette smoking, and marijuana use. Uncontrolled correlations indicated that religious attendance in every school year (9th through 12th) was significantly and negatively related to substance use. Using cross-lagged path analysis and adjusting for control variables, researchers found that religious attendance was uniquely related to lower rates of substance use, whereas involvement in non-religious club activity was not. Thus, the evidence is clear that religious involvement is related to less substance use/abuse in Christian-majority populations.

Psychosis

The relationship between religiosity and psychotic illness is complex, since severe mental illness gives rise to psychotic symptoms that are often manifested by religious delusions or hallucinations. In this case, it is the mental illness that is driving the pathological expression of religiosity, not religiosity driving the mental illness. This makes cross-sectional correlations difficult to interpret. Our systematic review uncovered 39 studies that examined religiosity and psychotic symptoms in Christian-majority samples. Of those, 10 (26%) found fewer psychotic symptoms in those who were more religious, 9 (23%) reported more psychotic symptoms among the more religious, and the remaining studies found either no association (29%) or both positive and negative associations (21%) depending on the particular religious characteristic measured.

Psychological Well-being

While the majority of studies find less emotional and mental disorder among those who are more religious, the relationship between religiosity and positive emotions is even stronger. Of 301 studies in Christians that examined R/S and well-being, happiness, or life satisfaction, 237 (79%) reported positive relationships. Only three (1%) reported negative relationships. With regard to hope, of 39 studies, 29 (74%) found positive relationships and none reported negative relationships. For optimism, 25 of 30 studies (83%) in Christian-majority populations reported positive relationships and no studies reported negative relationships. Finally, 41 of 44 (93%) reported significant positive relationships between R/S and meaning or purpose in life. More recently, in a meta-analysis of results from 75 independent studies examining 66,273 adolescents and young adults examining the relationship between religiosity/spirituality and a wide variety of mental health outcomes, including psychological well-being, Yonker and colleagues (2012) reported the average effect sizes across studies was +0.16 for well-being/happiness (p<0.001). We also found in a cross-sectional study of 132 persons with major depressive disorder (62% Protestant) that while religious involvement was unrelated to depressive symptoms, there was a strong relationship between religiosity and positive emotions (p<0.0001) (Koenig et al., 2014). Thus, religious involvement in Christians is associated with positive emotions in the vast majority of studies.

Locus of Control

An internal locus of control is the extent to which a person believes they have control over their own destiny by the personal decisions they make. In contrast, those with the an *external* locus believe they are helpless to direct their lives and that powerful other people or institutions are in control of their future. It has long been known that those who have an internal locus of control experience better mental health.

The belief that "God is in control" is not usually included as an example of an external locus of control, although some may interpret it this way. Instead, belief that God is in control is actually an indicator of internal locus of control, since the person believes that God is in control of their futures (not powerful humans or institutions). There is also a specific measure called the God Health

Locus of Control Scale that tries to determine the extent to which one believes that God is in control of one's health (or more specifically, that God empowers the individual to take control of their health). Most of the research, however, has not used measures that distinguished an "external local of control" from a "God locus of control," which has made some of the findings difficult to interpret.

At least 20 studies have examined the relationship between religiosity and locus of control in Christian-majority populations. Of those, 12 (60%) reported a greater sense of personal or internal control among those who were more religious or spiritual. Only 3 studies (15%) found significantly lower control among the more R/S.

Personality Traits

Researchers have also examined the relationship between religiosity and personality traits, which are lifelong patterns of how people relate to themselves and others. Personality traits tend to have a biological component that is rooted in genetic predispositions, so such traits may or may not be easily influenced by religious involvement. Personality traits are often assessed using the "Five-Factor Model" that examines five aspects of personality: extraversion, neuroticism, conscientiousness, agreeableness, openness to experience. I now summarize the research on religiosity and these five personality traits, limiting that research to Christian-majority populations.

Extraversion. Extraversion is a positive psychological trait associated with being more outgoing, talkative, and energetic in social situations when relating to others. Introverted persons are those at the other end of the spectrum who tend to be more inner focused, reflective, and less socially outgoing. Of 46 studies in Christian-majority populations, we found that 18 (39%) reported that those who were more religious were more extroverted (compared to 3 studies or 7% that reported less extraversion).

Neuroticism. Neuroticism reflects an enduring tendency toward anxiety, worry, brooding rumination, fluctuation in mood, and feeling uptight. These individuals are often self-conscious and do not cope well with stressful situations. Of 51 studies in Christian-majority samples, most (61%) found no relationship between neuroticism and religiosity or spirituality, 12 (24%) reported lower neuroticism among those who are more religious, and 5 studies (10%) found more neuroticism in those who were more religious. These findings contrast with those reported by Sigmund Freud who described highly religious persons as suffering from an obsessional neurosis (Freud, 1927).

<u>Conscientiousness</u>. Persons who are conscientious tend to be well organized, efficient, self-disciplined, productive and successful. This contrasts with the less conscientious person who tends to be laid back and less goal-oriented, and may be at higher risk for antisocial or criminal behavior as they attempt to "cut corners" and avoid work. Of 28 studies, 19 (68%) found that religiosity in Christians was associated with significantly greater conscientiousness, while only 1 study (4%) reported lower conscientiousness and this finding was only among males in the sample.

<u>Agreeableness</u>. Those who are more agreeable tend to be cooperative, considerate, and attentive to the needs of others. They are characterized by being more trustworthy, honest, and nice when described by others. Of 28 studies in Christians, 24 (86%) reported a significant positive relationship between agreeableness and religiosity, and no studies found a significant negative relationship.

<u>Openness to Experience</u>. This personality dimension involves a preference for variety and new experiences. These individuals tend to reject traditional or conventional ways and prefer doing things "outside the box," driven by their intellectual curiosity and tendency to question norms. Of 24 studies in Christian-majority populations, 10 (42%) found that religiosity or spirituality (more often spirituality) was associated with significantly greater openness to experience, whereas 2 studies (8%) reported significant negative relationships. Both of these last two studies measured traditional or conservative religious beliefs as their religiosity indicator.

Social Health

By social health, I mean number and quality of social interactions, availability of support from friends and relatives, degree of marital satisfaction and stability, and the absence of antisocial, delinquent, or criminal behavior.

<u>Social Support</u>. Of 70 studies identified in our systematic review conducted in Christian-majority samples, 58 (83%) reported that those who were more religious experienced greater social support. No studies found lower social support among those who were more religious.

Marital Satisfaction and Stability. This measure of social health assesses the stability of marital ties (absence of divorce or separation), degree of marital satisfaction, and degree to which a person treats their spouse with respect and care (vs. emotional or physical abuse). Of 75 studies, 64 (85%) reported greater marital satisfaction, less divorce or separation, and less spousal abuse among those who were more religious. Again, no studies reported less marital satisfaction or lower stability in those who were more religious.

Antisocial Behaviors. Finally, 99 studies examined delinquency or criminal behavior and religiosity in Christian populations, with 74 (75%) finding significantly less antisocial behavior in those who were more religious or spiritual, 5 reporting a nonsignificant trend in this direction, and only 2 studies (2%) indicating more crime or delinquency in the more religious.

Summary of the Research

The majority of quantitative studies in this systematic review found that religious involvement among Protestant-majority Christian populations is related to less depression, greater self-esteem, less suicide, less anxiety, less alcohol and drug use/abuse, greater psychological well-being, greater conscientiousness, more agreeableness, and better social health. Not all these studies are high quality, the vast majority is cross-sectional, and confounding factors are not always controlled. There has been accusation of bias in the reporting of results, with researchers making claims that go beyond the data (see Sloan et al., 1999, for methodological critique, and Koenig et al., 1999, and Benson et al., 1999, for rebuttals). Given the difficulty in obtaining funding support to conduct large well-designed studies on religion and mental health (since the National Institutes of Health and other secular funding bodies are reluctant to support such research), most studies have been carried out with only minimal resources and often with none at all. However, well-designed observational research (including those that have prospectively followed large samples for many years) and randomized clinical trials, while much fewer in number, tend to confirm the findings reported by the many more cross-sectional studies. This research supports causal associations between religiosity and mental health, although relationships are likely to be bi-directional such that religiosity not only affects mental health, but mental health may also affect religiosity. Recent research, often with better methodology than earlier studies, has in general reported similar findings.

In summary, this research does not indicate that religious involvement by Protestant Christians is always associated with good mental health, and there are certainly many individual cases where the exact opposite is true. However, there is a lot of evidence indicating that Protestant beliefs do not in general have negative effects on mental health, and a moderate amount of evidence suggesting these effects are in the positive direction.

CHAPTER 8

CLINICAL APPLICATIONS

What, then, does the mental health professional, pastoral counselor or clergy do with this information? The suggestions I make below are based on the evidence from research, 35 years of clinical experience providing counsel to Protestant Christian clients, and a whole lot of common sense when addressing something as personal and sacred as a person's religious faith. But, first, let us consider the case below.[1]

Case Vignette

> Jeff experienced a back injury as a result of a car accident about six months ago. This forced him at age 40 to stop work and go on disability due to limitations in his mobility. Since then he has required multiple back operations, with minimal return of functioning. Besides the physical disability, the accident and surgeries that followed left him with chronic pain unrelieved by muscle relaxants, high-dose gabapentin, various nerve

---

[1] Details of this case have been altered to protect the identity of the individual being discussed

stimulation devices (both superficial and implantable), and even narcotic pain killers (which his pain was not responsive to due to its neuropathic nature). He was now experiencing severe shooting pains into his hip and legs virtually day and night, and was told by doctors at the chronic pain clinic that there was not much more they could do. Jeff's depression worsened and he soon began contemplating suicide. As a result, his psychiatrist placed him on a combination of antidepressants and low dose benzodiazepines, and encouraged him to see a psychologist to help him cope with the pain.

On initial evaluation, the psychologist (who was Jewish) took a spiritual history. He discovered that Jeff was a religious man and member of a large conservative Protestant congregation. He also learned that Jeff was a deacon in his church, and when the pain was not too severe, would go out with other deacons to visit people around the neighborhood "witnessing" to them. Jeff told the therapist that his faith in the Bible, role in the church, and his family were the only things that stopped him from committing suicide. The psychologist decided to treat his depression with standard cognitive behavioral therapy, but one that was sympathetic to and supportive of his religious faith. After three months of therapy, Jeff continued to feel depressed on and off as the pain waxed and waned, but his suicidal urges lessened as he continued to remain engaged in his church and use his faith to give meaning to his life, both of which his therapist strongly supported (despite having different beliefs than Jeff). This included the therapist listening respectfully and gently tolerating Jeff's efforts to convert him.

Given the large amount of observational research and numerous clinical trials reviewed above that document the benefits that religious involvement has on mental health in Protestant Christian-majority populations, several clinical applications flow naturally from these findings.

1. Take a Spiritual History
A primary task of the clinician, whether or not a religiously-integrated approach to therapy is considered, is to take a detailed spiritual

history in order to identify the client's religious beliefs (or lack thereof) and the role those beliefs and practices play in the patient's mental health and psychopathology. Not only is this necessary to provide respectful mental health care in the context of the Protestant patient's belief system, but also in deciding on whether those beliefs are a resource or a liability. In cases where religious beliefs appear to be a liability standing in the way of progress, further consultation will be needed with someone who is an expert in the patient's faith tradition (and perhaps co-therapy conducted with that person).

A detailed mental health spiritual history in Protestant clients should include the following information, divided here into general information about the client's religious beliefs and more specific information related to their particular Protestant tradition.

General information:
- the importance of religion to the patient currently[1]
- their religious environment during childhood and importance to parents
- current level of involvement in faith community
- use of religious beliefs to cope with current circumstances
- religious practices of particular importance to client
- client's perspective how religion may be contributing to current problems or distress
- any religious/spiritual experiences that have significantly affected client's life in past
- importance of religion to members of family and support network
- concerns that mental health treatments may conflict with religious beliefs
- family and faith community's support of client's seeking mental health care

---

[1] If not important, this ends spiritual history for now. However, the mental health professional may circle back to the spiritual history again later after a therapeutic relationship has been established in order to gather the information listed above. This should be done slowly over time, without pushing too hard if the client resists (although effort should be made to gently identify the sources of resistance, since these may relate to the client's current psychopathology). Collecting this information is particularly important if religion has been important to the client in the past and there has been a change; reasons for change, then, need to be explored.

Protestant-specific information:
- Protestant denomination currently affiliated with
- Protestant denomination raised in
- approximate date/age when became member of denomination
- history of a religious conversion experience
- nature of conversion experience (sudden vs. gradual) and precipitating factors
- if conversion sudden, whether this occurred during period of emotion instability
- beliefs about the Bible and importance to client
- beliefs about God/Jesus and if consistent with their faith tradition
- beliefs about Salvation
- concerns about their Salvation or relationship with God/Jesus
- feelings about living up to expectations of their Protestant beliefs
- support received from members of their Protestant congregation

Armed with this information, the mental health professional is now ready to proceed with a mental health care plan in the context of the client's Protestant faith background.

2. **Provide a Safe Place**

Provide a friendly and safe place where clients can talk freely about their religious faith, good or bad, without judgment. Maintain a respectful, interesting receptive attitude at all times to the client's Protestant faith (whether the person is currently active or not, whether he or she speaks well of it or not).

3. **Guilt**

Listen for feelings of excessive guilt over real or imagined transgressions. Don't try to immediately rationalize or remove the guilt; rather, seek to understand it better from the client's faith perspective. Identify core beliefs that may be driving the guilt but be careful in overtly challenging religious beliefs.

4. Non-Religious Protestant Clients

If the client is not actively religious, then the mental health professional should proceed with secular psychotherapy that is respectful of their personal and cultural beliefs. Aggressive attempts to reconnect the person to his/her Protestant faith tradition should be avoided. If the client was once religious and has now become socially isolated or is despairing for lack of meaning in life, the therapist might gently ask if the client has considered re-establishing connections with their faith community (or a different one). The therapist may help the client weigh the plusses and minuses of such re-involvement, but again following the client's lead.

5. Utilize Faith Resources

If the client is religious, but not a candidate for religiously-integrated therapy or does not prefer this approach, then the therapist should provide secular psychotherapy that is supportive and respectful of the client's religious beliefs. There may be times during secular psychotherapy, though, when the client's religious beliefs may be utilized to support changes in attitude and behavior. In-depth knowledge about those religious beliefs, though, is usually necessary.

6. Consider Religiously-Integrated Therapy

If the client wishes to have therapy from a religiously-integrated approach, then the mental health professional must decide on whether he or she is qualified to provide this type of therapy or needs to refer the client to someone with these qualifications (e.g., a certified pastoral counselor[1]). An evidence-based Christian form of religiously-integrated cognitive behavioral therapy (CBT) for depression has been developed that relies heavily on Biblical scriptures consistent with Protestant beliefs (Koenig et al., 2015; Pearce, 2016). A therapist manual for this form of Christian CBT and both patient and therapist workbooks, along with a training video, are freely available on the Duke University's Center for Spirituality Theology and Health website (CSTH, 2014).

---

[1] In the United States, this may be a member of the American Association of Christian Counselors or a local Samaritan counseling center (for conservative Protestants), or of the American Association of Pastoral Counselors or Association of Professional Chaplains (for mainline or liberal/progressive Protestants).

7. Challenge/Re-Educate

If the client's Protestant beliefs are contributing to their psychopathology, and this is confirmed following consultation with an expert in that particular Protestant denomination, then the following approach is suggested. First and foremost, the mental health professional should inquire about and listen respectfully, learning as much as possible about the role that religious beliefs are playing in supporting psychopathology. Gathering as much information as possible about the natural history of how religion became intertwined with the mental condition is the therapist's goal. This must be done in an open and receptive manner and without confrontation (at least during this initial information gathering stage). There will come a time, once the therapeutic relationship is firmly established and the patient feels safe and accepted, when gradual, gentle, and persistent Socratic questioning may help to guide the patient towards a more "healthy" use of their Protestant beliefs. Emphasis here is placed on gradual, gentle, and persistent within an atmosphere that is safe and comfortable. Arguments over religious beliefs will almost always be unsuccessful and will adversely affect the therapeutic alliance.

8. Be Supportive and Neutral

Whether religious resources are utilized in therapy or not, be supportive of the Protestant religious beliefs/practices the client finds helpful (or might find helpful in the future as a way of coping with emotional issues, but do so from the client's perspective). If the client is receptive and open to healthy religious practices, and these are not clearly pathological, then they may be encouraged; if the client shows any resistance, don't push. However, as with non-religious clients, it may be informative to gently explore where the resistance is coming from in a future session. Never give clients the impression that they are not religious enough, since they probably get plenty of that from family and fellow church members. Whether it is a psychiatrist prescribing biological therapies or a therapist providing counseling, the mental health professional should be viewed by the client is neutral, interested in, open to and supportive of the client's Protestant faith, but always on the client's side and never judgmental. The same applies to clergy who are counseling members of their congregation.

CHAPTER 9

SUMMARY AND CONCLUSIONS

Protestant and Catholic beliefs/values are very similar and (in general) positively related to mental health, which has been documented by a large and growing research literature. However, there are also distinct differences between Catholics and Protestants. The particular Protestant beliefs will depend on where persons fall along a spectrum from fundamentalist to conservative to mainline to liberal/progressive in their theology. Since there are 30,000+ Protestant denominations worldwide, only a careful spiritual history can determine where the patient falls on this spectrum. When religion is only marginally important, many Protestants will do fine with standard secular therapy. For those in whom religion is important, the mental health professional's goal will be to provide psychotherapy that is respectful and supportive of the patient's particular Protestant beliefs. In some cases, a religiously-integrated form of therapy may be considered if the patient is religious, a candidate for religiously-integrated therapy, and prefers this approach. In cases where Protestant beliefs are intertwined with or even responsible for psychopathology, the therapist should follow a sensitive, gradual, informed, and strategic approach as described briefly above.

REFERENCES

Ankerberg, J., & Weldon, J. (2012). *Protestants & Catholics: Do They Now Agree?*. ATRI Publishing.

Bainton RH, Nelson EC, Spalding JC, Chadwick WO, Marty ME (2016). Protestantism. *Encyclopedia Britannica*. Retrieved from https://www.britannica.com/topic/Protestantism (accessed on 2/9/17)

Barrett DB, Kurian GT, Johnson TM (2001). *World Christian Encyclopedia: A Comparative Survey of Churches and Religions in the Modern World* (2nd edition). New York, NY: Oxford University Press

Beliefnet (2001). Fasting Chart: Fasting across religions. Retrieved from http://www.beliefnet.com/Faiths/2001/02/Fasting-Chart.aspx (accessed on 3/8/17)

Benson H, Cohen HJ, George LK, Koenig HG, McCullough ME, Myers DG, Post SG, Worthington EL (1999). Exploring links between religion/spirituality and health: Position statement. *Scientific Review of Alternative Medicine*, 3 (1): 52-55

Bruce S (1985). Authority and fission: The Protestants' divisions. *British Journal of Sociology* 36(4):592-603

Byrd A (2016). Adventist Healthcare: A view from the top. *Spectrum*, May 13. Retrieved from http://spectrummagazine.org/article/2016/05/13/adventist-healthcare-view-top (accessed on 2/7/17)

CSTH (2014). *Religiously-Integrated Cognitive Behavioral Therapy (RCBT) Manuals and Workbooks* (including training video). Durham, NC: Duke University Center for Spirituality, Theology and Health. Retrieved from http://www.spiritualityandhealth.duke.edu/index.php/religious-cbt-study/therapy-manuals (accessed on 1/22/17)

CSTH (2017). *Center for Spirituality, Theology and Health Newsletter* (research updates 2010-2017). Durham, NC: Duke University. Retrieved from https://spiritualityandhealth.duke.edu/index.php/publications/crossroads (accessed on 2/9/17)

Dunn J (2001). Giving in different denominations. *Philanthropy Magazine*, published by Philanthropy Roundtable. Retrieved from http://www.philanthropyroundtable.org/topic/excellence_in_philanthropy/giving_in_different_denominations (accessed on 3/8/17)

Exline, J. J. (2002). Stumbling blocks on the religious road: Fractured relationships, nagging vices, and the inner struggle to believe. *Psychological Inquiry*, *13*(3), 182-189.

Ezzy, D. (1993). Unemployment and mental health: a critical review. *Social science & medicine*, *37*(1), 41-52.

Fides, SLA (2016). Catholic Church statistics, 2016. *Zenit: The World Seen from Rome*, October 23. Retrieved from https://zenit.org/articles/catholic-church-statistics-2016/ (accessed on 1/30/2017)

Freud, S. (1927). Future of an Illusion. In Strachey J (editor and translator), *Standard Edition of the Complete Psychological Works of Sigmund Freud*. London: Hogarth Press, 1962.

Furnham, A. (1984). The Protestant work ethic: A review of the psychological literature. *European Journal of Social Psychology*, *14*(1), 87-104.

Gallup Poll (2013). Most Americans practice charitable giving, volunteerism. *Gallup*. Retrieved from http://www.gallup.com/poll/166250/americans-practice-charitable-giving-volunteerism.aspx (accessed on 3/9/17)

Glass, J., & Levchak, P. (2014). Red States, Blue States, and Divorce: Understanding the Impact of Conservative Protestantism on Regional Variation in Divorce Rates 1. *American Journal of Sociology*, *119*(4), 1002-1046.

Good M, Willoughby T (2011). Evaluating the direction of effects in the relationship between religious versus non-religious activities, academic success, and substance use. *Journal of Youth & Adolescence* 40:680-693

Diffen (2017). Catholic vs. Protestant. *Diffen.com*. Retrieved from http://www.diffen.com/difference/Catholic_vs_Protestant (accessed on 2/2/2017)

Koenig, HG (1998). Religious beliefs and practices of hospitalized medically ill older adults. *International Journal of Geriatric Psychiatry* 13:213-224

Koenig, HG (2004). *Faith and Mental Health: Religious Resources for Healing*. Conshohocken, PA: Templeton Foundation Press

Koenig, HG (2006). *In the Wake of Disaster: Religious Responses to Terrorism and Catastrophe*. Conshohocken, PA: Templeton Foundation Press

Koenig HG, Idler E, Kasl S, Hays J, George LK, Musick M, Larson DB, Collins T, Benson H (1999). Religion, spirituality, and medicine: A rebuttal to skeptics. *International Journal of Psychiatry in Medicine* 29:123-131.

Koenig, H.G., King, D.E., Carson, V.B. (2012). *Handbook of Religion and Health*, 2nd ed. NY, NY: Oxford University Press

Koenig, H.G., Al Shohaib, S. (2014). *Health and Well-Being in Islamic Societies*. NY, NY: Springer

Koenig HG, Berk LS, Daher N, Pearce MJ, Belinger D, Robins CJ, Nelson B, Shaw SF, Cohen HJ, King MB (2014). Religious involvement, depressive symptoms, and positive emotions in the setting of chronic medical illness and major depression. *Journal of Psychosomatic Research* 77(2):135-43

Koenig HG, Pearce MJ, Nelson B, Shaw SF, Robins CJ, Daher N, Cohen HJ, Berk LS, Belinger D, Pargament KI, Rosmarin DH, Vasegh S, Kristeller J, Juthani N, Nies D, King MB (2015). Religious vs. conventional cognitive behavioral therapy for major depression in persons with chronic medical illness: A pilot randomized trial. *Journal of Nervous and Mental Disease* 203(4), 243-251.

Koenig HG (2016). Association of religious involvement and suicide. *JAMA Psychiatry* 73(8): 775-776

Koenig HG (2017). *Catholic Christianity*. Amazon: CreateSpace Publishing Platform

Li S, Okereke OI, Chang SC, Kawachi I, VanderWeele TJ (2016). Religious service attendance and lower depression among women - A prospective cohort study. *Annals of Behavioral Medicine* 50(6):876-884

Lindberg CH, Crow PA, Fredericksen L, Hick J, Spender S, Sullivan LE, McGinn BJ, Benz EW, Wainright G, Chadwick H, Pelikan JJ, Hogg WR (2016). Christianity. *Encyclopedia Britannica*. Retrieved from https://www.britannica.com/topic/Christianity#toc67461 (accessed on 2/9/17).

Maselko J, Hayward RD, Hanlon A, Buka S, Meador K (2012). Religious service attendance and major depression: a case of reverse causality? *American Journal of Epidemiology* 175(6): 576–83.

Pearce, MJ. (2016). *Cognitive Behavioral Therapy for Christians with Depression: A Practical Tool-Based Primer*. Templeton Foundation Press.

Pew Research Center (2011). Global Christianity – A report on the size and distribution of the world's Christian population. *Religion & Public Life*, December 19. Retrieved from http://www.pewforum.org/2011/12/19/global-christianity-exec/ (accessed on 1/30/2017)

Pew Research Center (2014a). Religious Landscape Study (RLS-II). *Religion & Public Life*. Retrieved from http://www.pewforum.org/religious-landscape-study/frequency-of-prayer/ (accessed on 3/8/2017)

Pew Research Center (2014b). Religious Landscape Study (RLS-II). *Religion & Public Life*. Retrieved from http://www.pewforum.org/religious-landscape-study/attendance-at-religious-services/ (accessed on 3/9/2017)

Pew Research Center (2014c). Religious Landscape Study (RLS-II). *Religion & Public Life*. Retrieved from http://www.pewforum.org/religious-landscape-study/frequency-of-reading-scripture/ (accessed on 3/9/2017)

Pew Research Center (2015a). The future of world religions: Population growth projections, 2010-2050. *Religion & Public Life*, April 2. Retrieved from http://www.pewforum.org/2015/04/02/religious-projections-2010-2050 (accessed on 1/30/2017)

Pew Research Center (2015b). America's changing religious landscape. *Religion & Public Life*. Retrieved from http://www.pewforum.org/2015/05/12/americas-changing-religious-landscape/ (accessed on 2/3/17)

Rasario MD (2014). 7 key differences between Protestant and Catholic doctrine. *Hendricks Center for Christian Leadership and Cultural Engagement*. Retrieved from http://www.dts.edu/hendrickscenter/blog/7-key-differences-between-protestant-and-catholic-doctrine-del-rosario-mikel/ (accessed on 1/6/17)

Rauschenbusch, W (1917). *A Theology for the Social Gospel.* New York, NY: Abingdon Press

Schuster, M. A., Stein, B. D., Jaycox, L., Collins, R. L., Marshall, G. N., Elliott, M. N., et al. (2001). A national survey of stress reactions after the September 11, 2001, terrorist attacks. *New England Journal of Medicine* 345(20):1507-12.

Sethi, S., & Seligman, M.E.P. (1993). Optimism and fundamentalism. *Psychological Science*, 4, 256-259.

Sethi, S., & Seligman, M.E.P. (1994). The hope of fundamentalists. *Psychological Science*, 5, 58.

Sloan, R. P., Bagiella, E., & Powell, T. (1999). Religion, spirituality, and medicine. *Lancet* 353(9153):664-667

Smith, T. B., McCullough, M. E., & Poll, J. (2003). Religiousness and depression: evidence for a main effect and the moderating influence of stressful life events. *Psychological Bulletin*, *129*(4), 614.

Trepanowski, J. F., & Bloomer, R. J. (2010). The impact of religious fasting on human health. *Nutrition Journal* 9(1): 57

VanderWeele TJ, Li S, Tsai AC, Kawachi I (2016). Association between religious service attendance and lower suicide rates among US women. *JAMA Psychiatry* (formerly *Archives of General Psychiatry*) 73(8):845-851

Yonker JE, Schnabelrauch CA, DeHaan LG (2012). The relationship between spirituality and religiosity on psychological outcomes in adolescents and emerging adults: A meta-analytic review. *Journal of Adolescence* 35:299-314

ABOUT THE AUTHOR

Harold G. Koenig, M.D., M.H.Sc., completed his undergraduate education at Stanford University, nursing school at San Joaquin Delta College, medical school training at the University of California at San Francisco, and geriatric medicine, psychiatry, and biostatistics training at Duke University Medical Center. He is currently board certified in general psychiatry, and formerly boarded in family medicine, geriatric medicine, and geriatric psychiatry, and is on the faculty at Duke as Professor of Psychiatry and Behavioral Sciences, and Associate Professor of Medicine. He is also Adjunct Professor in the Department of Medicine at King Abdulaziz University, Jeddah, Saudi Arabia, and in the School of Public Health at Ningxia Medical University, Yinchuan, People's Republic of China. Dr. Koenig is Director of the Center for Spirituality, Theology and Health at Duke University Medical Center, and has published extensively in the fields of mental health, geriatrics, and religion, with over 500 scientific peer-reviewed articles and book chapters, and nearly 50 books in print or preparation. His research on religion, health and ethical issues in medicine has been featured on dozens of national and international TV news programs (including ABC's World News Tonight, The Today Show, Good Morning America. Dr. Oz Show, and NBC Nightly News), over a hundred national or international radio programs, and hundreds of newspapers and magazines (including Reader's Digest, Parade Magazine, Newsweek, Time, and Guidepost). Dr. Koenig has given testimony before the U.S. Senate (1998) and U.S. House of Representatives (2008) concerning the benefits of religion and spirituality on public health, and travels widely to give seminars and workshops on this topic. He is the recipient of the 2012 Oskar Pfister Award from the American Psychiatric Association and the 2013 Gary Collins Award from the American Association of Christian Counselors.

Made in the USA
San Bernardino, CA
09 May 2018